Greater Than a Tourist Book Series Reviews from Readers

I think the series is wonderful and beneficial for tourists to get information before visiting the city.

-Seckin Zumbul, Izmir Turkey

I am a world traveler who has read many trip guides but this one really made a difference for me. I would call it a heartfelt creation of a local guide expert instead of just a guide.

-Susy, Isla Holbox, Mexico

New to the area like me, this is a must have!

-Joe, Bloomington, USA

This is a good series that gets down to it when looking for things to do at your destination without having to read a novel for just a few ideas.

-Rachel, Monterey, USA

Good information to have to plan my trip to this destination.

-Pennie Farrell, Mexico

Aptly titled, you won't just be a tourist after reading this book. You'll be greater than a tourist!

-Alan Warner, Grand Rapids, USA

Thank you for a fantastic book.

-Don, Philadelphia, USA

Sergiu Miron

Great ideas for a port day.

-Mary Martin USA

Even though I only have three days to spend in San Miguel in an upcoming visit, I will use the author's suggestions to guide some of my time there. An easy read - with chapters named to guide me in directions I want to go.

-Robert Catapano, USA

Great insights from a local perspective! Useful information and a very good value!

-Sarah, USA

This series provides an in-depth experience through the eyes of a local. Reading these series will help you to travel the city in with confidence and it'll make your journey a unique one.

-Andrew Teoh, Ipoh, Malaysia

Tourists can get an amazing "insider scoop" about a lot of places from all over the world. While reading, you can feel how much love the writer put in it.

-Vanja Živković, Sremski Karlovci, Serbia

GREATER THAN A TOURIST – TIMIȘOARA, ROMANIA

50 Travel Tips from a Local

Sergiu Miron

Sergiu Miron

Greater Than a Tourist
Visit our website at www.GreaterThanaTourist.com

Lock Haven, PA

ISBN: 9781980272342

>TOURIST

50 TRAVEL TIPS FROM A LOCAL

Sergiu Miron

BOOK DESCRIPTION

Are you excited about planning your next trip?
Do you want to try something new?
Would you like some guidance from a local?

If you answered yes to any of these questions, then this Greater Than a Tourist book is for you.

Greater Than a Tourist-Timişoara, Romania by Sergiu Miron offers the inside scoop on Timişoara. Most travel books tell you how to travel like a tourist. Although there is nothing wrong with that, as part of the Greater Than a Tourist series, this book will give you travel tips from someone who has lived at your next travel destination.

In these pages, you will discover advice that will help you throughout your stay. This book will not tell you exact addresses or store hours but instead will give you excitement and knowledge from a local that you may not find in other smaller print travel books.

Travel like a local. Slow down, stay in one place, and get to know the people and the culture. By the time you finish this book, you will be eager and prepared to travel to your next destination.

Sergiu Miron

TABLE OF CONTENTS

18. The Merlin Puppet Theater
19. The Rozelor Park
20. The TimiȘoara Botanical Park
21. The Children's Park
22. The TimiȘoara Zoo
23. The Student Complex
24. The Epic Club
25. The D'arc Club
26. The Jazzisimo Pub & Lounge
27. The Ambasada Café & Bistro
28. The Manufactura Handmade Cafe Club
29. The Daos Club
30. The TimiȘoreana Beer Factory
31. The Curtea Berarilor Pub & Restaurant
32. The Scârț Loc Lejer Bar
33. The Sky Restaurant
34. The Merlot Restaurant
35. The Old House Restaurant
36. The Caruso Restaurant
37. The Dinar Restaurant
38. The TimiȘoara Tram Restaurant
39. The Iulius Mall/Shopping City TimiȘoara
40. Exit Games (Escape Room Adventure)
41. The MagTehnica Indoor Shooting Range
42. The TimiȘoara Paintball Club
43. The Red Motor Go-Karting

DEDICATION

This book is dedicated to the love of my life, my fiancée Daniela.

Sergiu Miron

ABOUT THE AUTHOR

Sergiu Miron is a Romanian writer who lives in Timişoara, Romania and loves to write and spend time with his family. He has lived in Timisoara for the last 10 years so he has a good understanding of what the town has to offer. He has visited all the places mentioned in this book and he wholeheartedly recommends all of them.

Sergiu loves to travel whenever he has the chance and is often visiting Germany for business reasons and its neighboring countries for leisure. Traveling has always been a part of his life so he has visited most countries in Europe and a couple of countries in Asia. He is fluent in English, speaks German at a conversational level and is always happy to meet new people and expand his knowledge through interaction with novel ideas, concepts, and mentalities. Traveling has made him kind, sociable and has given him a better understanding of the way the world works at an interpersonal level.

Sergiu Miron

HOW TO USE THIS BOOK

The Greater Than a Tourist book series was written by someone who has lived in an area for over three months. The goal of this book is to help travelers either dream or experience different locations by providing opinions from a local. The author has made suggestions based on their own experiences. Please do your own research before traveling to the area in case the suggested places are unavailable.

Sergiu Miron

FROM THE PUBLISHER

Traveling can be one of the most important parts of a person's life. The anticipation and memories that you have are some of the best. As a publisher of the Greater Than a Tourist book series, as well as the popular 50 Things to Know book series, we strive to help you learn about new places, spark your imagination, and inspire you. Wherever you are and whatever you do I wish you safe, fun, and inspiring travel.

Lisa Rusczyk Ed. D.
CZYK Publishing

Sergiu Miron

OUR STORY

Traveling is a passion of the "Greater than a Tourist" series creator. Lisa studied abroad in college, and for their honeymoon Lisa and her husband toured Europe. During her travels to Malta, an older man tried to give her some advice based on his own experience living on the island since he was a young boy. She was not sure if she should talk to the stranger but was interested in his advice. When traveling to some places she was wary to talk to locals because she was afraid that they weren't being genuine. Through her travels, Lisa learned how much locals had to share with tourists. Lisa created the "Greater Than a Tourist" book series to help connect people with locals. A topic that locals are very passionate about sharing.

Sergiu Miron

WELCOME TO
> TOURIST

Sergiu Miron

INTRODUCTION

"The impulse to travel is one of the hopeful symptoms of life."
Agnes Repplier

Timișoara is the largest city in the western part of Romania. This city has a long, winding history, dating back to the 12th-century. The city passed through the hands of rulers from the former Kingdom of Hungary, the Ottoman Empire, the Austro-Hungarian Empire and finally the Romanian administration. The Austro-Hungarian Empire's beautiful baroque building style has earned Timișoara the nickname "Little Vienna". As part of Timiș County and the larger Banat area, Timișoara has much to offer to its tourists: everything from museums, exhibitions, cafes, parks, restaurants and cultural events for people looking for a more refined experience to clubs, vibrant nightlife, sport and outdoor activities for the thrill seekers.

The city is a combination of areas bustling with life and motion, adjacent to quiet parts of town that serve as oases of tranquility for those who seek them. Timișoara is a city of contrasts; new and old meeting and melding together in harmony or clashing in almost seizure inducing architectural battles. The same goes for the interaction between mentalities of the old and new generations living together.

Sergiu Miron

1. THE CITY CENTER

Another name for it is Victoriei Square. At one end of the square, you will find the National Romanian Opera while at the other you will find the Orthodox Cathedral towering over the city. There are two promenades left and right of the central green area. One is called "Corso," formerly used by gentlemen and ladies of the high society to leisurely take their strolls, while the other is called "Surogat" and was used by those belonging to the working class. You are only allowed to run on the Surogat.

Almost all of the buildings in the square are built in the baroque style with the ground floor turned into restaurants, cafes or stores. In the summertime, all the cafes and restaurants have terraces set up outside the store that stays open until the late hours of the night. Concerts, open-air exhibitions, and seasonal markets take place here. The square is populated from morning until evening, making it a very good place to meet new people, socialize and get acclimated to the city and its rhythm

2. THE TIMIȘOARA STRONGHOLD

The first historical mention of a fortified city can be tracked as far back as the 14th-century. Since its placement was strategic, it faced much turmoil over the ages, being conquered by the Romanians, the Turks, and the Austro-Hungarians before finally landing under the custody of the Romanian government. When the Austro-Hungarians besieged the Turkish-controlled fortifications in 1716, the walled city was completely destroyed in the skirmish only to be rebuilt in the Pagan style, much bigger and better fortified, becoming a stronghold. Towards the end of the 19th-century, progress in weapons development, particularly artillery has rendered the walls ineffective against sieges.

By that time the fortifications were hindering the growth of the city. As a result, the city's walls were torn down and the moats were filled. At present, all that remains of the stronghold is the Huniade Castle, the Theresia bastion, and preserved portions of the wall and bunkers sprinkled throughout the city central area.

3. THE THERESIA BASTION

Theresia is the last bastion still standing from the time of the Austro-Hungarian rule over Banat. As part of the multi-layered defense walls, it was built in the baroque style. This side specifically, used to be a grain storage area. After the defense walls were torn down, the bastion was left intact as a reminder of the past. Even so, after many years of neglect from the authorities, it was in bad shape so, in 2010 it receives a full restoration and the inner yard is transformed into a posh half-open courtyard with restaurants, cafes, and galleries artfully embedded in the old walls.

There are many exhibits being shown in rotation linked to the history of the bastion. Also, medieval music concerts are being held in the courtyard as well as the occasional medieval mock-fight performed by enthusiasts fully dressed in accurate replica armors. This is a more high-end location where the young and rich of the city meet in a wonderful location where the concept of "the old meets the new" is done right. Strict regulations have obligated the store owners to tastefully include their businesses in the preexisting structure without introducing too much contrast in the building style

4. THE UNIRII SQUARE

This is the oldest square in the city, built in the baroque style, matching all its surrounding buildings. Flanking its sides are the Roman Catholic Dome, the Baroque Palace, and the Serbian Orthodox Cathedral. There you can also find the Canonic Houses, the Lion House, and the Palace of the Orthodox Diocese. Near them are the Scont Bank, the Elephant, and Three Husars houses. All of these buildings line the square and are in harmony with the baroque style making for a nice oasis of architectural beauty.

Right in the middle of the square stands the Holy Trinity statue, also known as the Plague Column, as a reminder of the Plague epidemic that devastated the Banat area between 1731 and 1738. Between the Plague Column and the Roman Catholic Dome is a fountain that offers its thirsty visitors mineral water. On the sides of the square at ground level, there are numerous cafes that feature open terraces in spring, summer, and autumn (with heaters).

The place is bustling with life all throughout the day and is a nice spot to spend an afternoon or an evening, considering the multitude of social and cultural events often happening place there

5. THE LIBERTĂȚII SQUARE

Go through Victoriei Square past the Romanian National Opera and you will come across Libertății Square. Right in the middle of the ripple-like cubic stone pavement rests the statue of the Holy Ioan Nepomuk and the Virgin Mary wearing a crown of stars and holding a lily in her hand, the symbol of purity.

A little to the side is another much more recent statue, of an oversized boy with square-shaped cut-outs all over his body, holding his hand to his head like you would hold a phone and gazing upon the much older sculpture with an air of indifference. The image speaks volumes over the attitude of the younger generations towards culture.

In one of the corners of the square is the Atlantean House, a neoclassic built structure with strange sculptures of "Atlanteans" (mythological men living in the kingdom of Atlantis) with elongated tails spanning over half of the height of the building and supporting the roof with their heads.

The piazza is lined with benches on both sides of the busy promenade so this is the perfect place for people watching or just taking a break from all the sight-seeing and trying to figure out who is that statue trying to call

6. THE ORTHODOX CATHEDRAL

Across Victoriei Square, on the opposite side of the National Opera, stands the Orthodox cathedral. In 1919, when the region of Banat (a large area formerly belonging to the Austro-Hungarian Empire that includes Timiș County) was annexed to Romania, a strong symbol of the presence of Romanians in Timișoara was desired by the ruling parties. The local parish organized a fundraiser for building a church in 1926. By 1936 the funds necessary for erecting a cathedral that had a capacity of 5000 people were mostly there.

The cathedral was finished in 1956 because of WWII that halted the construction for several years. The Orthodox cathedral overlooks the city at 90 meters high with its 11 towers and 7 large church bells and is one of the tallest orthodox churches in the world. The architecture blends Moldavian and Byzantine influences with Banat style floors. The cellar houses an icon exhibition and a religious art museum.

The steps outside the main entrance are famous for being the starting point of the Revolution of 1989 that freed Romania from communism and its dictator, Nicolae Ceaușescu

7. SAINT GEORGE'S CATHEDRAL

Catedrala Sfântul Gheorghe, as it is known in Romanian, also goes by the name of the Roman Catholic Dome and was finished in 1774. The structure rests at one end of Unirii Square. The baroque building style of the Austrian master builders makes this Dome one of the most culturally significant buildings in Timișoara. The edifice is built of brick and stone. The two steeples have a reduced height because the builders thought that making them too large would turn the cathedral into a target for the catapults and later cannons of invaders, due to the placement of Saint George's Cathedral near the defensive wall of the stronghold that used to exist there.

The interior is lush and exuberant with 9 altars crafted in baroque and rococo style, an Austrian organ that sounds fantastic and beautifully sculpted statues all around. The acoustics in the cathedral is very good so occasionally concerts are being held inside. People attend the Holy Mass regularly and the Dome is frequented by the Hungarian and German minorities since the liturgy is held in 3 languages: Romanian, Hungarian and German

8. THE STRONGHOLD SYNAGOGUE

The stronghold synagogue is just a synagogue that was built in the former Timișoara stronghold. The structure is built in an eclectic style with Moorish influences. This is one of the more exotic buildings in the city. The combination of different building styles highlighted by the Moorish subtle finishes and the use of multiple building materials for the structure itself and the decoration is a treat to the eyes.

In the period between the two world wars, there were approximately 13000 Jews in Timișoara that dwindled to a mere 600 in the present. After the Second World War, most of the remaining Jews immigrated to Israel, so in 2001 the building was donated to the Timișoara Philharmonic Orchestra for a period of 50 years.

A concert at the synagogue, be it rock, blues or symphonic, is an unforgettable experience due to the unusual location and stunning acoustics

9. THE TIMIȘOARA NATIONAL OPERA

Located in Victoriei square, opposite from the orthodox cathedral, this is a state institution entertaining its guests with operas, ballet, and theater. Domestic and foreign shows run on a regular basis with emphasis on the great classics. The building has played a significant role in the 1989 revolution as the gathering point of the revolutionaries.

Nowadays this baroque interior establishment enchants the guests with formal evenings and professionalism in the production of shows. This is a good location for culture enthusiasts and people looking to have a nice time while going out. The location is central and there are shows almost every day of the week

10. THE BANATUL PHILHARMONIC

The Philharmonic was grounded in 1871 and is composed of an orchestra, a chorus, and various soloists. Going to the Philharmonic has always been a treat for me. I only went there on special occasions and was pleased by the performance every time. There are a variety of events happening at the Philharmonic, from concerts to exhibitions.

Lately, the managers have decided to be more open to modern additions to their musical repertoire and also allowing prestigious bands to perform on their stage, the most recent being The Dire Straits.

It goes without saying that this spot is for connoisseurs, for those that appreciate the beauty of classical music played in its natural environment.

There is an order to be followed when going to the Philharmonic, the proper attire is required, and I love going through the motions and experiencing the feeling of accomplishment when I manage to blend in with the high society that normally frequents these events and enjoy a beautiful rendering of a classical piece of music played live

11. THE HUNIADE CASTLE

Standing as a proud historic monument, the Huniade Castle is also the oldest building in the city, built in the early 14th-century. Just like the stronghold it used to be part of, the castle has been destroyed and rebuilt many times, its function also changing from the residence of a king to suitable lodging for royalty passing through, to barracks for artillery.

Today it houses the Banat National Museum with its impressive collection of archaeological objects found in Banat such as the Neolithic Sanctuary from Parța (a unique monument in Europe). The museum consists of the Natural Science section, the Archaeology and Restoration sections.

The Archaeology department has over 350000 items from the Paleolithic to the modern era, partly displayed in 19 museum halls. The Natural Science department offers its visitors permanent exhibitions such as "The evolution of life forms," "The evolution of man" and "Banat flora and fauna" in the form of micro-diorama, unique in Romania. One of the more unusual permanent exhibitions entails the violin collection of Dr. Cornel Şuboni, with impressive violins such as an Amati from 1616 originating from Cremona, Italy

12. THE BANAT VILLAGE MUSEUM

This museum is the only one of its kind in Romania, accurately replicating the core of a traditional Banat village from the 19th century. The "civic center" of the village is composed of a Townhall, a church, a school and of course, a pub. The museum is placed at the outskirts of the city so no modern structures (other than the tarmac alleyway) are going to ruin that feeling of being in a quaint, small village.

All the buildings have been purchased from villages around the Banat area and reassembled using the original materials and building techniques from the 19th century. The structures are fully furnished and tooled up. Some of them are used as workshops with employees offering to teach visitors how to craft small objects with simple tools, how to use various objects common around the household.

Since the year 2000, in an attempt to integrate the cultural particularities of the minorities living in Banat, the German house, the Slovak house and the Hungarian house have been inaugurated. The Banat Village museum hosts a series of festivals that honor traditional culture and occasional traditional markets where handcrafted items, from pottery to elaborate wooden sculptures are being sold

13. THE ART MUSEUM

The Baroque Palace, situated in Unirii Square, houses this museum. There are over 8000 pieces of art in total, in the form of paintings, sculptures, decorative and graphic art.

One of the main exhibitions is that of Romanian painter Corneliu Baba with more than 80 paintings displayed, spanning over his whole career. The contemporary art department displays the different artistic styles that have been popular in the Timișoara art community. The Banat folk art department houses religious icons made mostly of wood with wood paintings scattered throughout, originating from local and national workshops and also from Russian and Greek workshops, dating back to the 18th and 19th-century. The European art department is one of the most important exhibits, with most paintings being of Italian origin

14. THE KINDLEIN MUSEUM

Colloquially known as "the biggest small museum", it is one of the few private museums in Timisoara. This project was initiated by the Kindlein family and it runs independently from public funding. The central idea here was to accurately display the jeweler and watchmaker workshop of Petru Kindlein, an entrepreneur who was active in the first half of the 20th century.

The exhibition presents the furniture and specialized tools, advertisements, documents, photos and objects used in that time period but the real eye-catcher is the clock collection comprised of pocket watches, grandfather clocks, and other special timepieces. The museum also offers workshops for children and sometimes adults, introducing them to wood sculpting with metal inserts

15. THE COMMUNIST CONSUMER MUSEUM

This place is different from other museums. Located in the basement of the Scârț Bar, it depicts a typical Romanian apartment from the communist period where locals have every chance of encountering an object from their childhood or teen years.

The initiators of this project have started gathering common objects found in communism and placed them in 4 rooms: a living room, a bedroom, a children's room and a kitchen. While the place is advertised as looking as somebody could live there, in reality, it looks like a level of a hidden object game: every nook and cranny is packed in an orderly fashion with communism memorabilia. The best part about it is that you are allowed and even encouraged to snoop through all the drawers, closets and stacked objects to discover things you might have missed by just politely looking around.

The best time to visit the museum is in the morning when all the objects are neatly organized because, by the end of their working hours, the place looks like a hoarder's home. I believe it is an interesting throwback to a time when life was very different in Romania, shown from a working-class perspective that is covered in nostalgia

16. THE LLOYD PALACE

Found in the Victoria Square, it is known as "the most beautiful house in Timișoara". The edifice was built in 1910-1912 in the Secession style of architecture (Art Nouveau).

The building stands 3 stories high. On the ground level, you can find "Lloyd Restaurant and Cafe", the place where the most important high-class citizens used to socialize

17. THE HYDROELECTRIC STATION

"The Turbine" as it is called, is a hydroelectric power plant located on the Bega river, that has been in use for over 100 years and is considered the most valuable piece of industrial architecture in Timișoara.

Besides providing electrical energy, the station also solved the problem of damp cellars and flooding in the neighborhood. The building is interesting on the outside with a tower rising on one side while the inner workings of the plant are hidden away in the lower portion. A visit inside reveals the engine room fitted with 600 horsepower Ganz Villamossagi Rt turbines roaring away and producing electric energy.

There is also a wooden bridge on the downstream side that allows for a clear view of the river. This is a good choice for history and antiquated industrial machine enthusiasts who want to see an old piece of machinery in proper working order. The owners have recently opened up the doors of the facility for public viewing every Sunday

18. THE MERLIN PUPPET THEATER

In an era where just about everything relating to entertainment can be seen by turning on the TV or the computer, a puppet theater seems to have little to offer as the predecessor to our current era of televised fun. That is not entirely true. While it cannot compete with its successors in the special effects department, a puppet show has its own charm and lures those watching to use their imagination in helping to bring the characters to life.

The Merlin Puppet Theater is a public cultural institution that started running in 1947. There are over 20 puppet shows running in rotation at the moment. There are also other projects running occasionally involving animations, actors with masks or non-verbal plays. This spot is mainly meant for children and families looking to have a good time.

There is also an element of nostalgia associated with watching a puppet show, a throwback to the past for those who have already experienced something like that in their childhood and also an element of novelty for those who haven't

19. THE ROZELOR PARK

Also known as Rosarium or The Culture Park, it is one of the most beloved hangout spots in Timișoara. The landscaping work done in 1929, meant to reinvigorate the then bleak-looking park, changed the public garden's layout to an English style one with alleyways, baldachin's and round flower beds.

In the interwar period over 1200 species of roses were planted here and its name was changed to Rosarium. At the same time, an open-air theater was built that still stands today. In 1944 the park was destroyed by bombardments and later rebuilt.

Today, the public garden is host to different open-air shows, concerts, galas, exhibitions. This park is not as big as others but it is charming, with hidden benches for those desiring a little bit of privacy and is a good spot for meeting new people or just having a relaxing afternoon in the sun

20. THE TIMIȘOARA BOTANICAL PARK

Known as the Botanical Garden, the park was designed with dendrology in mind and started in 1996. At present, there are 219 plant species spread over 9.8 hectares.

The alleyways are meant for pedestrian use but also to divide the garden into 8 sectors, as follows: the plant systematic sector, the medicinal plants sector, the tropical flora sector, the ornamental sector, the Romanian flora sector (with 4 sub-sectors), the Mediterranean flora sector, the North American flora sector and finally the Asian flora sector.

The garden is visited by people interested in a nice, long walk among the changing variety of plants and also by those that want to have a nice picnic or sunbathe since it is allowed, provided they clean up after themselves. The park is located in a very central area, close to the old Timișoara stronghold ruins

21. THE CHILDREN'S PARK

The park was last renovated in 2012 and is a wonderful location for children and their parents. There are many attractions for the little ones: swings and slides in all shapes and sizes, a boat ride, trampolines. There are a magic castle, a pirate ship, and a ghost tunnel. Further in there is a carousel and a chessboard with large pieces. Hammocks and long chairs line part of the alleyway and a train tour goes through the park.

A day in the park is guaranteed to give kids an exciting time and parents a break. Beware though, and I speak from experience, the park is big and kids tend to run from one attraction to the other so temporarily losing them is a common occurrence. The premises are fenced up so even if they disappear they are sure to still be in the area

22. THE TIMIȘOARA ZOO

The newest zoo in Romania, the Timișoara Zoological Garden is located in the Green Forest, in the north-eastern part of the city and spans over a surface area of 6.34 hectares. The zoo was modernized in 2007, now exhibiting 16 habitats that are sheltering 29 species and about 144 animals. Over 1 million Euros has been invested in the new concept of the facility: "more space, closer to animals", greatly increasing the number of visitors and turning it to one of the favorite hangout spots of young people in the warm months of the year. In addition, the zoo shelters endangered species in a project meant to increase the chances of survival, reproduction and eventually release back into the wild of said species.

The entrance part of the zoo houses small pens with domesticated animals such as goats (big and small), ferrets and small deer. The visitors are free to pet the animals but not feed them ever since a couple of the animals died from eating food that did not match their diet. Further in await the bigger species such as deer, bears, Llamas. There are also monkeys, koi fish and all manner of birds, some of which are allowed to roam freely through the park (beware of the pelican).

A visit to the zoo is definitely worth it because of the laid-back atmosphere, the long, winding paths of the zoo with surprises around every corner and the clean, crisp air delivered by the surrounding forest

23. THE STUDENT COMPLEX

This is a neighborhood in Timișoara, centered on Universitatea de Vest (the state university) composed mostly of student dorms and small businesses erected in order to cater to the needs of students much like a student campus. There are a number of student pubs, clubs and restaurants and the clientele almost completely changes every 4 years.

The neighborhood is alive with students rushing in every direction, there is always something to do or see. Events are being organized at all hours of the day, drinking, eating and fun is constantly on the menu. Nobody knows the Student Complex neighborhood like its temporary residents so asking one of them for information is the easiest and most fun way of getting useful information and possibly a date.

The students are mostly friendly, open, they can speak English and if they have the time they will show you around provided you treat them with respect. The Student Complex can be a fun, crazy experience spent in the company of friendly students looking to show the people that they have acknowledged as friends (which isn't too hard, just buy them a drink) all that this neighborhood has to offer

24. THE EPIC CLUB

This is the newest, hottest club in Timișoara. The fun is guaranteed in a luxurious environment full of people that want to have a great time in this establishment. Be sure to wear your best Sunday clothes otherwise you won't get in. Entry is, of course, free for the ladies but men who want to feast their eyes on some of the most beautiful women Timișoara has to offer, have to pay.

The music is remixed mainstream style, done by an experienced DJ and guest appearances from domestic and foreign celebrities are a regular occurrence here. Everybody is on their best behavior and troublemakers don't even make it past the entrance. The guests are awesome, open to having fun and ready to get wild as the night goes on. The parties become epic sometimes. The people get in a celebratory mood and the club becomes an awesome place to be. That explains why the entrance line is so long and why a table reservation is a must.

The employees speak English so you won't have any problems with communication. Luxury doesn't come cheap so expect to pay a little more than in the other clubs for the reservation and drinks. Beyond that, if you want to have a good time on Saturday night, this is the place to go

25. THE D'ARC CLUB

This is one of the oldest clubs/cafes/pubs in Timișoara and an old watering hole for the artists and the artistically gifted in the city. The establishment is located in the Theresia bastion. The appeal of this place lies in the diversity of people walking through its doors and the different types of vibes that you get when going there on multiple occasions.

During the day, this is a normal cafe with everything that is expected from a coffee shop. The transformation happens in the evening and during the night hours when the place comes to life in ever-changing forms depending on what type of event takes place. The D'arc club prides itself on originality and constantly tries to surprise its guests with live music in the mainstream and indie genres, thought-provoking exhibitions and nightclub attractions.

The place is packed on weekends and is a good choice for those who like to dance really close to strangers, which is allowed in this location. Also, the variety and uniqueness of the people found there can lead to very interesting encounters and conversations

26. THE JAZZISIMO PUB & LOUNGE

The name speaks for itself. There is an air of elegance in the Theresia bastion based club that I have seldom encountered. The place is small, accommodating 150 people but is full of character. From the large photos of Marilyn Monroe and Humphrey Bogart draping the walls to the small objects resting comfortably on the bar and window sills, this place screams, well, whispers elegance.

The focus is on quality and culture. You can expect to find anything from live jazz music to a carefully chosen movie being projected on the wall. The acoustic is fantastic thanks to the owners investing an absurd amount of money in the sound system which, according to them, is one of the best in the world. Jazz fans are welcome here and much of the lounge's repertoire revolves around this music genre but in the last years, they have expanded their musical horizons in other directions as well.

The guests are nice, sociable, bilingual and eager to take part in interesting conversations. As a closing note, the men are in for a pleasant surprise when going to the toilet in the Jazzisimo Pub & Lounge

27. THE AMBASADA CAFÉ & BISTRO

At its core, Ambasada is a cafe and bistro. That, however, is not the reason it has found its way on this list. The idea of the Ambasada owners is to offer a location to people with the initiative like freelancers, musicians, sculptors, basically all kinds of artists and also companies and Non-governmental organizations to express their ideas and make them a reality as long as the ideas serve the common good.

That means that Ambasada houses many exhibitions, workshops, and training in a multitude of areas of interest, concerts and movie nights. Those activities change frequently so there is always something new to see. What appealed to me were the open-minded people I encountered there, ready to teach me what they knew without trying to act superior.

The atmosphere is great, new faces are welcome and immediately accepted and integrated, the subjects are diverse and most interesting and the mindset and openness of the organizers to what is new and exciting are contagious. This place is worth a visit if only for the element of surprise

28. THE MANUFACTURA HANDMADE CAFE CLUB

This one is another doozy. The club is nice by day and heavy metal by night. The members of the staff have crafted all the furniture in the club and the idea is that if you want, you can take a piece of furniture, a painting, a mug or an ashtray home with you, as long as you pay for it.

During the day, this is a nice, quiet club that hosts workshops and exhibitions of handmade-whatever with the possibility of purchase. The music is chill, the people are relaxed. In most weeknights, the establishment offers its guests a good place to have a drink and mingle. The atmosphere is relaxed, suited to a cafe.

The craziness starts in the weekend (and on some weeknights) around dusk when heavy metal bands take the stage and start blasting away. The nice cafe turns into the booming club, the clientele changes and long-haired heads start banging to electric guitar chords and heavily struck drums. This club has a multiple personality disorder

29. THE DAOS CLUB

The club opens in the evenings from Wednesday until Sunday. This establishment is meant for concerts. The stage is taken by bands playing rock, post-rock, alternative rock. There are also concerts of hip-hop, electronic music, and reggae. This is the definitive small-scale concert experience.

The bands are not so well-known outside the devotees' circle, but they sing their heart out. The audience goes crazy at times, pulsating as a single organism to the beat and encouraging or overpowering the band with noise, but all of that belongs to the experience of going to the Daos club. Those that can get into that mesmerized audience groove will have a great time.

With the space being restricted and the audience area being packed, I sometimes get the feeling that the event is much bigger than it actually is, with sound reverberating off the walls and back to the stage or the audience putting everyone in a state rhythmic euphoria

30. THE TIMIȘOREANA BEER FACTORY

This factory is first mentioned in the annals of Timișoara Stronghold in the second half of the 18th-century, built out need since there was a lack of drinkable water at the time. The brewing process of the beer ensured that all microbes and viruses present in the water were eradicated thus making beer an everyday drink for almost everybody, including children at the time.

Nowadays the factory produces the local brand of beer called Timișoreana that is distributed all over the Banat area. This factory has its own fresh beer tasting/dining hall area located in a renovated ballroom nearby. This building has kept the subtle nuances of the turn of the 19th-century charm, with long wooden tables, memorabilia on the shelves and large wooden beams spreading across the ceiling and the walls.

While the atmosphere is beautiful, it would mean little without beer fresh out of the adjacent factory. There is also food, but it serves as a garnish to the types of beer: Lager, Ale, Pilsner, Porter, and Stout. I personally recommend the unpasteurized beer, delivered 2 days after being brewed and with a shelf life of only 14 days which ensures that when you order, you know it is fresh

31. THE CURTEA BERARILOR PUB & RESTAURANT

This is a subsidiary restaurant to the Timișoreana Beer Factory, located in a fairly central area in a renovated prison building with its own inner courtyard that is fitted with sturdy beer benches and tables accommodating well over 100 people. There are 3 large rooms and a bar inside. The service is much more professional than in the dining hall of the Timișoreana Beer Factory and in addition to all the fresh beer and other mainstream alcoholic beverages being served, the food menu is much more varied.

There are two equally sized inner rooms with a seating capacity of 100 people each and a smaller room, a bit hidden away for a more intimate experience, available also for private events, with a seating capacity of 40 people. The atmosphere is always great here, with people from all walks of life meeting and mingling, eating well and drinking.

The waiters are constantly making beelines to the bar, bringing glasses and beer mugs in different sizes. The most popular order is 1 meter of beer: a 1-meter long wooden board with an indentation in the middle that fits beer mugs one near the other. I have a great time every time I go to Curtea Berarilor because the service is fast, the food and drinks are good, and the laughter of your neighbors is contagious after a few fresh beers

32. THE SCÂRȚ LOC LEJER BAR

To say that this bar is different is an understatement. First off, its cellar houses the Communist Consumer Museum. The other floors are also unique. While it gives off a faint communist aroma, this bar has a different vibe. Surreal, like an unintelligible dream, the elements placed throughout are at the same time well integrated and incompatible.

The name could be translated as Squeaky, casual place. When the bar first opened, the building was nearly unfurnished. The owners asked the clients to bring old furniture or interesting objects from home in exchange for free drinks. The idea worked so well that today, the bar looks like a surreal painting. The ceiling is covered in opened up umbrellas, the walls have bottles, paintings and signs hung up, in an apparently disorderly fashion that somehow works to bring the customer in a calm state of mind. There is a backyard with tables set up right near hammocks where the guests can relax and have a drink. All in all, this is a spot worth visiting. Words do not do it justice

33. THE SKY RESTAURANT

Located in the City Business Center on the 6th floor, this restaurant offers its visitors a panoramic view of the city and a select place to spend a delightful couple of hours surrounded by the elite of the city. This is one of the more high-end restaurants on this list and it caters to the needs of those who expect true professionalism in all aspects of the dining experience.

First off, the restaurant has a modern, elegant style blended in the urban look of the whole building. There are large windows from the floor to the ceiling allowing clients to see the city from a reasonable elevation. There is also a terrace with glass railings where people can dine in style above the noisy, bustling city below.

The food is fantastic. The menu is varied and expertly prepared by experienced chefs who take pride in what they do. The sommelier recommends the proper choice of wine. The prices are reasonable for the quality offered and the service is top-notch. This is one of my favorite locations for a stylish dinner

34. THE MERLOT RESTAURANT

A little bit outside the central area of town, in an old baroque building, is the Merlot restaurant. Warm, inviting and stylish, it surprised me in its simplicity and good taste. The dining area is covered in warm beige colors with well-placed lighting that serves to further enhance that cozy yet elegant feeling, the accompanying music is played at just the right level and the service is impeccable.

The best appetizer I have ever had in my life was a Parmigianino-covered pate served with freshly baked baguettes in this restaurant. The food was incredible. The menu is chosen from the French and Italian cuisine and the talent of the chef really shines through the wonderful dishes. I ate in silence not because I did not enjoy my company but because I couldn't stop long enough to entertain a conversation.

I have only been to the Merlot restaurant once but I was very pleasantly surprised. From the classic look of the establishment and the pleasant atmosphere to the exquisite cuisine and flawless serving, this is a restaurant definitely worth a try

35. THE OLD HOUSE RESTAURANT

This place reminds me of an old British gentleman's club. The feeling you get when you walk inside is unique. The interior is beautiful: large leather chairs around stylish hardwood tables, normal chairs with leather accents around dark-tinted tables. There are wood accents on the walls, a fireplace, old pattern wallpapers, very well-chosen. The furniture serves to set an atmosphere of a 1940s detective movie.

There are some modern elements sprinkled throughout the restaurant but they are not enough to take you out of the play-pretend mood you enter. This is a visual and imaginative journey in a place previously seen only in movies, fueled by looking left and right. For maximum effect, I recommend the smokers lounge. There is an open-air terrace but it looks normal.

As a plus, there is a children's room with toys. You can leave the kids there in order to enjoy a drink in peace. The food is alright but that is not the reason I go there. I go there to play, to pretend, to be a high aristocrat if I so choose

36. THE CARUSO RESTAURANT

Minimalist in style, this restaurant aims to focus the attention of the guests on the fine dining experience. The location is also carefully chosen, in the vicinity of the Theresia bastion, Libertății square, and the city center.

The appeal of this restaurant comes in the form of its dishes. While most eating places focus on traditional cuisine like French or Italian, the chef of this establishment has decided to go with an eclectic style, introducing fusion gastronomy as the differentiating element from other restaurants. While many try and fail, Caruso succeeds at combining cooking cultures and traditions in new ways with exciting results. The food is really good.

I tried traditional dishes in other restaurants and found them on the menu of Caruso. After a more careful inspection of the ingredients, I realized that they added a twist to the established recipe and decided to try it. I did not expect to be so pleasantly surprised. The change seemed insignificant to the untrained eye but the result was delightfully tasty

37. THE DINAR RESTAURANT

This Serbian restaurant is different, in that it takes the concept of a normal rustic establishment and infuses it with an overdose of rustic. Everything in this place except for the electric lights, the glasses, and the cutlery is rustic. Wooden floors hold big wooden tables with wooden benches. Wood walls support wood beams on the ceiling and the whole room is decorated with big wooden pieces from dismantled carts, other wood objects, and tools used around the house in the late 19th-century country home in the Balkans.

The place is a visual overload, an inundation of the sense of sight with warm wood tones that somehow, works. I can't explain it properly. I don't know why, but after a few minutes I settled into it and started feeling comfortable. The menu is varied, offering its clients a myriad of traditional dishes from the Balkan area mostly in big portions.

The big tables accommodate many people, the place can get loud, there are live bands occasionally playing traditional music. The people walking out usually hold or rub their bellies from the big portions. If that sounds good to you, visit the Dinar restaurant

38. THE TIMIȘOARA TRAM RESTAURANT

The mayor of Timișoara decided a couple of years ago to refurbish an old tram built in 1976 and equip it with tables, a toilet, a kitchen, and internet. In time, the tram came to be administrated by a company that offers occasional evenings of delight aboard the tram that follows the route of the first electric Timișoara streetcar.

The first guests go in close to dusk and a tour takes about one hour. When the tram arrives back at the starting place, the next batch of clients goes in. I went inside and I was pleasantly surprised by the violinist accompanied by a piano player spreading a mellow tune through the small space. The light was dim but pleasant. We were seated by the waiter who took our order and quickly brought us our food, politely informing us that we have just 1 hour before the ride is over.

We ate to the sounds of beautiful classical music playing in the background and a familiar and constantly changing scene as the streetcar made its way through the city. A timely reservation is necessary because the number of passengers is limited and the request for this service high, so make sure to plan this one out

39. THE IULIUS MALL/SHOPPING CITY TIMIȘOARA

I have put the 2 malls in Timisoara together because they offer a similar experience and the choice of going to one or the other is a matter of which one is closer. These shopping centers arc at a western quality level and offer products from a number of worldwide recognized brands as well as some domestic ones that rise to the accepted level.

They are very popular spots for locals of all ages, who choose to spend much time there shopping, eating at the food court, hanging out at the arcade, billiard or bowling area or training at the gym. The malls cater to those needs and keep bringing customers back. These are good places for people watching, hanging out at a cafe or strolling through the labyrinth-like construction (of one of them) in search of that perfect piece of garment or souvenir

40. EXIT GAMES (ESCAPE ROOM ADVENTURE)

There is a trend spreading across the world that has reached as far as Timișoara. I'm talking about the escape room phenomenon. I had heard about it in the past and imagined it based on my experience in playing video games belonging to that genre. While the games had given me a rough idea of what to expect, the experience in the Exit Games location, comprised of 3 rooms, was an altogether different beast.

First off, there is a time limit of 1 hour. That may sound like much, especially if you undergo the challenge with some friends and decide to divide the tasks, but ultimately this limit adds to the stress of the increasingly difficult tasks that need to be completed in order to escape.

You are given a brief introduction specific to the room you chose (Horror Hospital, Laboratory of Tesla or Mr. Bean-preparation for Christmas), the timer starts and then you are left inside to figure your way out. The first puzzles serve as accommodation to the style of the challenge, almost a tutorial, rising in difficulty as you progress only to get devilishly hard or ingenious towards the end. I don't want to give anything away because that would spoil the fun, just like playing a game with a walkthrough opened in another tab

41. THE MAGTEHNICA INDOOR SHOOTING RANGE

Gun enthusiasts will frolic. The indoor shooting-range is built at high standards and managed by experienced instructors. They offer training courses and assistance in all matters related to guns. They also offer guns, lots of them.

Some are iconic (Kalashnikov, Beretta, MP5), some I've never heard of, but all of them demand respect. Handling a gun is a big responsibility and being aware of how fast things can go wrong with a tool built specifically to kill cannot be stressed enough. You learn to respect the tool and its power. The instructors are patient, go through every step carefully and repeat a step if they feel you are not giving enough attention to a detail that seems insignificant at the time.

Shooting a gun is a powerful experience. The recoil on some of the guns is stronger than I expected, the sound so much louder and the targets so hard to hit. Shooting is a skill that I've yet to master. The establishment is very professional and modern, the guns are well maintained and the atmosphere is a relaxed kind of tense, like hearing laughter in between shots being fired from a shotgun.

42. THE TIMIȘOARA PAINTBALL CLUB

Paintball is awesome. You get to go there with your friends and have a couple of hours of adrenaline-fueled fun. The playing field is set up in an old military installation divided into levels so it's pretty much perfect. There are multiple levels to choose from with different obstacles, terrain, and objectives.

The fun lies in outsmarting your opponents with clever, well-coordinated tactical moves (that fail due to trigger-happy teammates) or just running in unprepared towards equally unprepared opponents and start shooting wildly hoping for that lucky headshot. There is a surprising amount of thought that needs to go into planning a winning strategy.

For the most part, my teammates ran around like headless chicken so we inevitably lost. Paintball is the closest you will ever come to a real gunfight (hopefully). The shots hurt but not so much that they take away from the fun and the experience and I believe this place is definitely "worth a shot"

43. THE RED MOTOR GO-KARTING

Go-karting is a fun sport. The vehicles, although small in size, deliver much power and are surprisingly agile. Combine this with a 6000 square meter indoor custom-built circuit and you have the recipe for a day of fun. The circuit is indoors, so that means you can go there and drive even if it's raining cats and dogs outside.

The circuit is secured with flexible PVC barriers all the way through and is relatively long (720 meters), with both long straights and technical portions. The beauty lies in mastering both and seamlessly gliding to the finish line. Go-karting is easy to pick up, hard to master.

I love everything about it, from gearing up, getting in the vehicle; racing like your life depends on it to the cold drink that serves as the trophy once you are done driving. There are 12 latest generation karts for adults and 13 for children, and training can and will be provided to those who need it. Men beware! This place is beginner-friendly and very addictive

44. THE MAXAIR FLIGHT CLUB

This company offers leisure flights with small aircrafts (the four-seat Cessna 172N that is, according to the employees, the most reliable aircraft ever built). The flights can be customized to the client's wishes regarding destination and length.

Most flights are executed over Timișoara, presenting a maximum of 3 guests with a beautiful aerial view of the city but if you want, you can literally fly to the other end of the country and back. The experience of flying in a Cessna is different from regular flights because the machine is small, agile and flies lower than commercial aircrafts allowing for a clearer view of the ground below

45. BALLOONY (HOT AIR BALLOON RIDES)

A balloon ride can be a special treat for that special someone or a new experience to add to the list. The hot air balloon accommodates up to 4 people or 400 Kg total guest weight. The rides start early in the morning at sunrise or a couple of hours before sundown if the weather and the wind allow it. The preparations start an hour before the flight and the guests are welcome to help unpack, spread out and inflate the balloon.

After lift-off, the contraption rises to a height of 1000 meters or more in a smooth, slow fashion. The balloon is in constant contact with a car following it on the ground so friends that fear heights can still be part of the experience via walkie-talkie from the jeep. After the landing, you get your "baptism" that entails receiving a "noble flying name," a diploma and a glass of champagne to celebrate the occasion.

The ride is silent except for the sound of the burner every now and then. There is a certified hot air balloon driver with you, but he keeps to himself and he is quickly forgotten in favor of the breathtaking view. As a precaution, you should bring some warm clothes with you since it can become chilly up there

46. THE LOVELOCK BRIDGE

The Pont des Arts Bridge in Paris is known because many couples went there, hung a lock and threw the key away as a symbolic gesture meant to reinforce the strength and durability of their relationship. Something similar can be found in Timișoara, a little-known fact even among the locals. Parallel to the Decebal Bridge, leading to the Children's Park is a smaller bridge over the Bega River, often overlooked because of its peculiar positioning. Somebody decided to hang a lock there and the news spread among the young people that have started filling the wire fence with their own declarations of fidelity.

I have hung a lock there with my girlfriend, threw the key away, and our love is still going strong. The act of pledging your loyalty to your loved one has a positive psychological impact on the relationship.

While the bridge still has a long way to go before it reaches the status of the Pont des Arts, this may be a good stop for couples to renew and reinforce their love for each other in an interesting and fresh way. All you need is a lock and a permanent marker

47. BOAT RIDES ON THE BEGA RIVER

The Bega River runs through Timișoara in a winding pattern and is relatively shallow, making naval travel possible only by small motor boats. There are 7 of them running commercial leisure routes up and down the river. The starting point is behind the orthodox cathedral, by the river (obviously). The rides start in the afternoon and end in the evening. Each tour takes 40 minutes to complete and you are brought back to the starting point.

The view is different from the boat. You move slowly through the bends and have time to take in the sounds and sights of the city or have a conversation with the other passengers. The atmosphere is relaxed and if you go on a boat with a tour guide he/she can also provide explanations in English regarding historical buildings on the way. This is a good opportunity for a change of pace or a break. The price of a ticket is symbolic and the ride is worth it for laid-back people

48. THE TERMALUM SPA

This is a location for weary travelers. As a spa, I consider it has everything that a person can wish for and then some. There are 2 medics on standby ready to make a professional assessment on the state of health of the guests (if they want to do that) and then recommend the appropriate treatments located in the facility.

They have 3 areas each offering specific treatments or methods of relaxation: the thermal area with hydro massage and thermal water coming from a deep underground spring, the spa area with saunas, massage rooms and relaxation rooms and finally the physical recovery area with specialized medical equipment for recovery. The Termalum spa is a great place for relaxation and the professional services provided are top-notch

49. THE UMT SWIMMING POOL

There are days when the weather is just perfect for sunbathing and a swim. Look no further than the UMT swimming pool. This place has everything: two pools with thermal water, two pools with normal water and a children's pool. This is one of the favorite spots for the locals in the summer.

The entry fee is symbolic but if you want a sun chair, it costs extra. There is also a food stand, a covered up bar for those who want to enjoy a cold beverage in the shade and a synthetic football field available for renting. The facility is large and also encompasses an event room and a spa fitted with all the latest technologies and gadgets meant to relax and beautify the clients.

This swimming pool is a good choice for active people, for those who want to swim and play in a safe environment, monitored by the lifeguards. The downside is that it can get crowded in the hot months of the summer and is loud. This is not a place for people seeking peace and quiet

50. THE MEHALA MARKETPLACE

This is the biggest market in Timișoara and consists of a car selling area and a bazaar-like part that sells everything under the sun. Going to the Mehala market is an experience, a different world altogether. The market is made up of stalls close to each other lining narrow, long pathways. A rudimentary roof system keeps customers dry when it rains. After you go in, you can spend hours looking at the merchandise displayed because there is much to see. You can find anything in there: tools, phones or clothes, you name it. There are auto parts, bikes fishing tools and so on.

The merchants expect you to haggle and will sell you the items you want for a much higher price if you don't. Most of the merchandise is counterfeit so don't be fooled into buying a 5 Euro pair of original Adidas shoes.

Beware of thieves! The narrow pathways and multiple exits provide a great environment for them. A little caution and common sense go a long way so if you are aware of your surroundings, you should be fine

Sergiu Miron

TOP REASONS TO BOOK THIS TRIP

Locals: They are friendly and welcoming.

Nightlife: Timișoara has great clubs, pubs, and cafes.

Food: The food is amazing in the right locations.

Sergiu Miron

> TOURIST
GREATER THAN A TOURIST

Visit GreaterThanATourist.com:

http://GreaterThanATourist.com

Sign up for the Greater Than a Tourist Newsletter:

http://eepurl.com/cxspyf

Follow us on Facebook:

https://www.facebook.com/GreaterThanATourist

Follow us on Pinterest:

http://pinterest.com/GreaterThanATourist

Follow us on Instagram:

http://Instagram.com/GreaterThanATourist

Sergiu Miron

> TOURIST
GREATER THAN A TOURIST

Please leave your honest review of this book on Amazon and Goodreads. Thank you. We appreciate your positive and constructive feedback. Thank you.

Sergiu Miron

NOTES